Sunflowers in Bloom

katarina illona

To my children -
you are everything.

I find inspiration in the idea of the sunflower. A magnificent work of art, this masterpiece stretches tall and proudly stands within whatever garden or field it finds itself in. Thick and sturdy, it has what it takes to be a survivor. To endure.

Looking always towards the sun, sunflowers face the light regardless of what is behind it. However, when there is no sun to be found, it turns to its neighbor in solace. (Or so people claim.) Whether or not this is true, what a beautiful concept this is: to turn to our loved ones when life is dark. When it seems as though the sun cannot be found.

Yet sometimes, they tire. They sag and droop, facing the earth. And that's alright. It's okay to be tired, to feel like you cannot go on. But don't let yourself be fooled: you're more capable than you think. Just because you're down doesn't mean you're out. You simply need some time to rest, so you can soon turn yourself back towards the light or the love of others.

As I write this, with my first-born baby sleeping in my arms, I realize how important this concept is. I strive to be like the sunflower. Not because they are sturdy and stand tall. (My dainty 4 foot, 10.5 inch self is the complete opposite.) But because they look for light despite the darkness and turn to one another for support. In a world full of sadness and pain, we must remain diligent, looking towards the light (and the good) while providing support to one another. Not only that, but we must allow ourselves to feel, express and process our feelings to find the way to move forward and grow.

After all, we have little ones to raise. To cultivate into kind, loving humans to take on this task when we no longer can. To ensure that, despite the negativity in our world, there is the chance for hope to bloom and love to flourish like a garden.

-katarina illona

Table of Contents

Light

It is important to look towards the light, just as the sunflower does. But, sometimes we must create our own light, enveloping ourselves in a light that nourishes and enriches our souls. Then, we can use that to encourage our sense of self.

To go far, to do great things.

View

Although the journey through life
is full of
the rollercoaster of highs and
lows -
when the highs occur,
no matter how far and few
in between,
I've come to love
and treasure the view,
grateful for when
I'll see it once more.

Hope

What a beautiful thing
hope is.
For something so small,
  vulnerable
  fragile
to have the potential to be
shaped into something
  powerful
  unmoving
with proper nurturing
guiding it to its true potential.
Even the strongest
have to start somewhere.
The Mighty Redwoods
   once started
as small saplings.

Peonies

Peonies may just be
my favorite example
of how
when you find the right moment
(or person)
and open up to the world,
there is unimaginable beauty
to be seen.

Wildflowers

Watching the wildflowers along the road
pass by
their soft, gentle colors
and silent presence
are a gentle reminder for me
that
everything will be okay.

Birthday Cake

Another year,
another candle on the cake
to brighten my way forward
and
help me see more easily
what is truly important
in life.

My Song

I sing the song of my struggles
to those who are willing to hear it.
Whose ears are always open,
not just when it is convenient for them.
Whose arms cradle me
in love and support,
time and time again -
urging me to continue
just when I think I can't go on.
I will never force anyone to listen to my melody,
especially when others make it obvious
they won't appreciate the notes or
understand the words.
I would rather mute myself,
halting the sounds and
censoring my own thoughts if it means
the right audience hears
what my heart is feeling.
So I'll keep singing my song,
to those with the love in their heart to listen,
while others are enveloped in silence.

Mindset

Cultivate a mindset
so beautiful,
as to make the sunset
    jealous.
Evoke the colors of the sky,
as you enrich the world around you
with your perspective.
Your palette could
paint someone's heart -
and just might
change the world.

Serendipity

Serendipity is just
a fancy way of saying
I finally caught a break.
That when the cookie crumbled,
it turned out to be a delicious
white chip macadamia,
flavored with decadent
white chocolate chips and
satisfied relief…
rather than the usual
deceiving culprit full of raisins,
parading as chocolate chips
despite being full of disappointment.
One day I will learn that
only rarely does the
cookie crumble in my favor.
But when it does,
I will savor it,
with a refreshing glass of milk.

Millionaire

I am a millionaire
in the ways that truly count.
My bank account is not stuffed to the brim
with zeros and commas,
but my heart is full to bursting with love.
My wallet is not thick
with wads of cash,
waiting to be spent
on trivial things.
Instead, my memory is crammed with
memories for me to treasure forever.
I might not have a vast net value
but to my loved ones, I am priceless.
Blessings rain down on me like
cash rains over CEOs.
So even though none of this
can pay my rent,
I am filthy rich in ways it truly counts.

Golden Glow

Sometimes, when the sun hits something just right, it is
illuminated in a golden glow of light. It almost
feels…magical! Like being enveloped in living sparkles. It is
important to treasure what makes you feel as though you are
enveloped in magic. Like you are empowered, embracing
yourself and what you contribute to the world.

Whatever prompts that feeling:
hold on to it and *treasure it always*.

Chess

Life is a game of chess.
You move one space,
inching your way ahead
    while I
move across the entire board -
leaving dust in my wake.
You may be a king,
    but I am a queen.

Fail

This will be the year
I may fail.
I will push myself
to the outskirts of my comfort zone
and crossover
into unknown territory.
I will attempt,
and I may fail.
But,
it means I *tried* -
I attempted
something new, something bold,
something I've never done before -
putting my bravest foot forward.
This will be the year
I might fail,
and it will be lovely.

Crush

Have you ever
had a crush on
someone you've never met?

I have.
Let me tell you about her.

She is strong
    showing kindness and courage
in the face of adversity.
Her smile can melt
    even the coldest of hearts.
She brings a joy
and a passion
for love and life
that cannot be captured
    in mere words.

She is a precious gem,
    a mighty queen,
She is
    pretty incredible and
    worth remembering.
    Deserving of love..

She is the woman I am becoming.

Fairy Tale

In stories
there is always a princess
    and
knight in shining armor -
but why can't I
be both,
tired of waiting for others
to rescue me.

It's time for me
to rewrite
the fairy tale ending
we've come to expect.

Taped

My heart has been
broken and shattered
more times that I'd
care to admit.

But still,
I've taped these
shattered pieces together,
to wear on my sleeves
so others can see
    I've loved.
    I've lost.
    I've kept going.

I wear my pieces
like a badge of honor.

Garden

My mind is a garden,
and my thoughts are the blossoms.
If I wouldn't let weeds grow
amongst the blooming life,
Why should I let them thrive in my mind?

Villain Arc

New Year means
   new possibilities
   new adventures
   new goals
but also,
   a new me.
I'm changing the narrative
   setting boundaries like margins -
bettering myself,
like a manuscript being edited,
adjusting the format
until I am better than ever.

It's a shame that to some,
this new chapter may read
like the start of my villain arc.

Store Bought

My favorite dress,
that makes me feel gorgeous,
empowered,
womanly,
was store bought.
My groceries,
nourishing the body
and helping me grow
were store bought.
My fashionable purse,
containing all the necessities
with which I live my life,
was store bought.
So -
What's the problem,
if my serotonin is store bought as well?
All the cool things apparently
come from there.

Puzzle

What I wasn't expecting
in life
was for the powers at be
to answer my cries,
my frustrations
and prayers
    with puzzles
    for me to solve on my own,
empowering myself along the way.

If you want something done right,
you might as well do it yourself -
and I'm a badass woman,
    who damn sure will.

Sleepy Girls

This one
is for all the sleepy girls.

For the bad ass, boss lady,
conquering the world
    girls.
The bossy, "talks too much",
running my mind to run the world
(and sometimes my mouth)
to get things done, problem solver
    girls.

It takes a LOT of energy
to slay
    all day.
So of course,
we're sleepy.

Slingshot

The harder you try
to hold me back,
the quicker I will shoot forward
a rubber band about to snap
launching myself above and beyond,
    all the way
    to the stratosphere.
You may as well call me
    Ricky Bobby,
because this slingshot is about to get
engaged.

Ghosts

I am surrounded by
the past versions of myself,
following me like ghosts.
Looking over my shoulder
I see glimpses of
who I used to be
wandering,
like lost souls,
no longer with a place in the world.
"You can move on", I tell them,
releasing each version of myself.
"You have served me well",
I tell them, grateful for
the lessons I've learned.
I wish them well,
letting them drift on the breeze
Like petals off a flower,
 "She loves me", I whisper
to each version that passes by.
Because I do.
They may be flawed, but
they are me.
and I love them for it.
Once my ghosts,
they are now my guardian angels,
protecting and guiding my growth
until I reach my best form yet.

Magnificent

I am the calm
before the storm.
My voice may shake
    like thunder,
my words flash like lightning,
warning of the conflict
at war within my mind.

I am the storm.
Feelings flashing,
emotions booming
swirling,
whirling,
until it seems like something's gotta give.

I am the brilliant rainbow
    trailing quietly after.
a shimmering collection of colors,
cornucopia of memories,
peace after turmoil
ready to give and accept love.

Cup

I know the contents of my heart
because I pour into it myself,
like a cup
overflowing.

Darkness

Sometimes, there is no sun. It's a cloudy day without the warm rays of light to be found. Likewise, there are times where we feel as though we have no sun. Allow yourself to have these off days, embracing and processing your feelings.

But, ensure you don't let these days overcome you. *You are incredible, after all.*

I'm Fine

How am I doing?

~~Life is exhausting.~~
~~It feels like a game of tag, but~~
~~instead of a gentle tap, I'm knocked~~
~~— onto the ground, struggling each time~~
~~— to lift myself back up.~~
~~Sleep eludes me, being plagued by nightmares~~
~~worrying of what is to come.~~
~~— Or not come.~~
~~Why do I bother? When it feels like fate~~
~~— has a personal vendetta out for me, when~~
~~— all I've done is share a smile and~~
~~— offer a kind word to strangers.~~
~~I cannot win, despite my hard work and~~
~~— determination to move myself forward.~~
~~I'm not sure how much more I can take.~~

I'm fine, thanks.
How are you?

Lexapro

Whoever said
"money can't buy happiness"
has never spent $1.20 a month
on 20mg Lexapro pills,
dulling the edge of
my sharp blade of worry -
constantly sharpening itself
on my own back.
How lucky they are to never have learned
their necessary dosage of happiness.

Searching

There must be
more to life
than looking for something,
constantly searching -
always gazing ahead to the next destination,
rather than enjoying the adventure
we experience along the way.
Life is supposed to be a journey
and not a destination.
But it's easy to get sidetracked,
and wonder
"Are we there yet?"
with our eyes facing only forward.

I'm Sorry

I'm sorry
that
this brain of mine,
as creative and magnificent
as it may be, still operates
with short circuiting wires
and repetitive processes.
That this complex machine
cannot simply "shut off".
No matter how desperately I wish, or
how hard I try.

I'm sorry
that
I get that I should just "not worry"
but this machine cannot process
that code.
Error 404.
No amount of 0's and 1's can
reprogram the exhausting
cycle I find myself in -
day in and day out.

I'm sorry
that
this thought is so
    excessive
    extensive
    regressive
    intensive.
If you think this is a lot,
I don't think you'd enjoy my mind.
Sometimes, even I don't.

I wish it didn't have to be this way.
I'm sorry
that
it's not so simple.

Tired

I'm tired.
There's a feeling deep in my bones
of not being "enough",
that can't be shaken off.
A deep dread, that smothers
my airways,
shrinking my lungs
until I don't think I can take much
more of being ignored,
of being pushed to the side,
like I don't matter.

I'm tired.
And no amount of naps
or sleeping can fix this.

Villain

Although
I may be the main character
a courageous heroine,
overcoming adversity
in my own thrilling story,
I cannot deny
there have been times
where I too
was a villain to myself,
plotting my own demise.

Breeze

Sitting outside,
I watch the leaves dance on the breeze
up
   up
      up
         and away
Until they are out of sight
And out of mind.

If only my worries did not weigh enough
to hold me down -
the weight of my troubles
pressing on my shoulders.
And instead, they could float away
   like leaves on the breeze.

Ink

A darker shade of black
could not exist
if I tried,
as I use my blood
to write feelings
across a
blank page.

Dining

Do not invite me
to dine at your table,
if respect will not be an appetizer.
If kindness is not available
as a side,
and joy is not there
to season my plate.
There is no need
to break bread,
if our mutual happiness
is not to be celebrated.
I am a picky eater,
but even this
shouldn't be too much to ask
for the dinner menu.

When

Can someone,
PLEASE someone,
ANYONE
tell me when I can
hit the switch.
Shut off the feelings,
dull emotions,
stop the pain from rising
and the anger from boiling.
Because this is getting to be
too much for one person to handle.

Armor

As I move forward,
I will hold on to the lessons
I've learned the hard way,
    every pain
    and heartache
wearing it like armor
as I forge ahead
in unchartered waters
of days to come.

Grief

Grief is a blanket.
I welcome the security and
sense of protection as it envelops me
like the arms of a old friend,
offering solace and support in the silence
but quickly becomes overwhelming
and sweltering.
I sweat under the warmth, but
cannot bring myself to shed the layer.

I welcome the sadness, a reminder
that I once held something so dear,
that it is worth missing, drawing happiness from
the memories that linger, always.
Yet,
I crumble with the realization that
that's exactly what it now means. Only memories.
The happiness you've inspired cannot
drown out the loss of your presence.
But
nor can the sadness destroy those precious moments
we have shared together, that are
engraved in my heart.

There is a give and take, with grief.
It takes so much from us
but, in its own twisted way,
gives peace in return.

Flames

There are times
when
the roaring flames of my fury
    overpower and override
the gentle flicker of kindness'
dancing flame in my heart.
And that's okay.
Fire burns
    but
    it also cleanses
        in the process -
there are some thoughts
that *need* to be
cleared from my mind
before they consume me wholly.

So let the
fire burn,
let it purge my toxic thoughts
as it clears the way
for the gentle flame
to move forward
little by little,
lighting my mind
and life,
with sparks of love.

Volume

We all know
that actions speak louder
than words.
But some forget
just how deafening
the silence
can be.
How the roar of nothing can
shake us to our core.
Especially from those
who
we'd expect to be heard.

Silence

Sometimes the deafening sound
of silence
is explanation enough.
When words lack volume,
yet contain strength enough
to still pack a punch.

Without uttering a word
you have made yourself
abundantly clear.

Sticks and Stones

We all know
how the old saying goes -
Sticks and stones
may break my bones,
but words will never hurt me.
Yet we never seem to remember
just how much
a few simple words can shatter
our sense of self
completely.

Pretty Things

Kindness blooms
all around us
    like beautiful flowers.
But our world is not kind
to pretty things,
and pretty hearts.

Light

How am I supposed to
shine my light
for the world,
to illuminate the path
for my children,
when it feels like
that light is dimming?
When it feels like
there is nothing left
but a sad spark
of false hope
as my light
drains to nothing.

Smothered

I know there
is more to life
than the feeling of insecurity
hanging over me
like a veil,
smothering, until I choke on
the feeling of hopelessness

more than the melodic symphony of
whispers in my head
tricking me, with
false reminders that
I
am
nothing.

I know there
is more to life than all of this,
but sometimes the weight of
my thoughts
is more than I can bear.

Flowers in the Garden

We are part of a big world, where each of us brings a unique beauty that comes together to form a beautiful garden of people. But sometimes our friends or family need a little extra sunshine and it's up to us to shine extra light on our flowers, to encourage them and their growth.

Madly in Love

I hope the next time
you fall in love,
it is with yourself.
The forever kind of love,
that stops time in its tracks
and shakes the earth on its axis.

I hope you never stop admiring
the gleam in your eye
and
the sparkle in your smile -
that rivals the stars in our sky.

I hope you always appreciate
the quirks that make you unique,
like flowers that bloom
in their own time,
making up a single part
of a breathtaking garden.

I hope you fall
madly in love,
and never look back.
Because the soul who deserves you,
sure as hell
isn't back there.

Lightbulb

How tragic it is,
that you do not realize
your worth.
That you
cannot see how
your smile lights a path
for those
wandering in the darkness.
You are
a lamp with which
to guide the feet of the lost.

Potential

Why is
the potential I see in you
deep down,
at such odds
with the person
you are willing to challenge yourself to be?

They don't have to be strangers -
if you would only hold yourself higher
than you limit yourself to believe
you are able to reach.

Alone

We do not celebrate alone.
Parties and celebrations share laughter and joy
"The more, the merrier!"
they say,
while we surround ourselves
with those we love
to lift ourselves and each other
to highlight the wonderful things
blessing our lives.

We do not celebrate alone.
So why do we make ourselves
suffer alone?

Heartbeat of the Town

Street performers. People talking.
Dogs barking. Seagulls cawing,
and waves lapping.
The daily heartbeat of the town,
reassures me that I,
and life,
are alive and well.

Blank Canvas

What good is a
new, blank canvas
if I'm
not able to fill it?
If I am not struck
by the consuming need
to document my thoughts onto
a tangible piece
I can cling to,
to reminisce with
for years to come.

To find something
worth doing everything I can
to cling to, forever.

Until
that person comes along,
the one who inspires meaning and
spectacular color in my world.
The one who
 jumpstarts my mind
and warms my heart,
like the reds, oranges
and yellows
burning the color wheel.

Stranger

I wish I knew who you are.

Wish I could understand the way you
shrug off a compliment
like a shirt itching your skin.

Why you push yourself down and
into the ground like
dirt trodden on -
while others are desperately trying
to lift you up.

Tell me why you hold yourself down
with weights of worry and ropes of sadness
when you are destined to soar.

I wish I knew who you really are.
Because the person I see in the mirror
is apparently a stranger to you.

Hustle and Bustle

There is a peaceful serenity in the
coming and going
of everyday life.
All around me,
people hustle and bustle,
going here
roaming there
surrounding me like a tornado.
But
in the eye of the hurricane
there is quiet.

(Or so Alexander said.)

Special Sunflower

Sometimes, someone truly special comes along to flip our
world upside down. To create more light, more of the magic,
that helps encourage and empower us. To change our life for
the better and brighten the world around us.

Turn to them when the world seems dark.

Our Love

Our love
is one for the ages.
A fairy tale,
brought to life
with magic breathed into
our souls,
entwining our hearts together.

Whatever you believe in,
whether it be
God, other beings,
the universe,
fate
or the stars -
No one can undo
the looping and twisting lace
our souls have become.

Under the Night Sky

My love for you
Is never ending,
Unyielding as the sun travels across the sky
and the moon regains its rightful place above us.

As the hands of the clock turn,
and the pendulum swings back and forth,
my heart continues to beat,
love never ceasing, no matter
if it is the early minutes before sunrise,
the hours creeping away in the sweltering afternoon
or the sunset, threatening to overtake the sky.

But,
my favorite time of loving you
is when we are bathed in the glow of the moonlight,
dark shadows enveloping us and
whispering their secrets of what tomorrow may bring.
When we can ignore that which may come,
and focus only on the here and now -
of you in my arms.

Shimmer

Let me bring a shimmer to your darkness,
enchanting the night with starlight -
chasing away the sadness
with remedies of laughter,
loving you until
no hint of doubt remains.

Engrave

Let me never forget
your smile,
the twinkle in your eyes
as you gaze upon my face
or
the feel of your touch dancing across my skin.

I will write your name in my heart,
engraving each letter carefully,
onto my soul -
pouring love into every etching,
that it may never disappear.

Vision

Memories of you
cloud my vision
    clinging to me,
a feeling that I can't shake.

Comforted by
the melody our laughter
    created together,
the sharp pain of your absence
becomes a dull ache.

I think back with a smile
and reminisce…
just a little something to take the edge off.

Language

We speak a language
that very few can understand.
Where silent conversations replace
    silent letters
and
stolen glances, words unspoken, replace
    proper pronunciation.
When a gentle touch doesn't need
to be conjugated
and
even a soft laugh can silence a racing mind.

Love is Strange

Love is perplexing.

It has turned me into a philosopher
Considering the reason of life
and why I was considered "worthy enough"
	for your affection
	and love, so pure.

My pondering, has started resembling that of a mathematician
certainly there is an equation for
	the good deeds I've done + kindness I've shown,
	multiplied by caring smiles I've shared with strangers
		To equal this good fortune I've found myself with.

Until I turn into a scientist,
exploring the cause and effect of my actions,
Analyzing a hypothesis that
	the cause of earning your attention,
		how I somehow managed to catch your eye -
	lead to the effect of having you
		forever by my side.

It has made me
	happy.

No matter what it inspires,
or what I ponder
I cannot deny
	that
love is strange.

Beautiful Love

I love…love.
Love is patient, love is kind.
And somewhere along the way,
as life ebbs and flows,
so does love.
It's a change we all notice
but not all appreciate.
Stolen glances and kitchen dances
become small acts that speak volumes
and thoughtfulness that
can't be understated.
Love is language, that
once learned,
will enrich your life.
A dance that
opens your eyes to
the beauty and power of
little moments.

How blessed am I
that my life has been made better
by a pretty beautiful love.

Sunflower Buds

Just as flowers grow and gardens flourish, every bloom must start from somewhere. Each one starts as a small bud, new to the world and ready to be nurtured, to grow into what they are *meant to be*.

For Levi

In the early hours of the morning
when the world is dark
and all around us rests,
I rock with you -
back and forth
back and forth
back and forth
the sound of your gentle breaths
it's own melody to soothe my heart.
Your tiny fingers grip my own,
and remind me that
at the end of the day,
my ability to survive
    is enough.

I am here
and that is all you need.

This Journey

I am not the same person
who started in this journey
nine long months ago.
I have grieved the loss of loved ones
    some now guardian angels, and
    some simply disconnected.
I have learned lessons about myself
and about others,
both difficult.
I have fallen, shattered,
    watched myself break into
    so many pieces that
I didn't think I'd come back together.
But like caring for the child I've so lovingly grown,
I take it day by day.
Week by week.
We have grown together,
creating a bond so unique and special.
But despite the frustration and pain I've felt,
I have been shown love and support,
    wrapped in loving arms of encouragement
    as cheers of
"You've got this Mama,"
warm my soul.

I am not the same person
who started this journey
nine long months ago,
and I am all the better because of it.

Lost and Found

Somewhere along the way
I lost myself and found something better.

Through the early morning feedings,
twilight hour rockings
and little hands that
grab not only my finger
    but my heart,
I managed to find someone new.
Someone nurturing,
cultivating of new life
and ready to fiercely protect it.
Someone who,
despite feeling desperately overwhelmed
will find a way
to run the race.

I mourn the person I was -
late night reading into the
early morning, leading to
    lazy mornings in bed,
carefree adventures and unlimited scrolling.
Yet,
this has turned into late night feedings
that shift into to early morning cuddles,
giggles that flip my heart
upside down and
fill my soul.
I celebrate the person I have become.

The me I lost was grand,
but this new me is even better.

Frozen

I wish I could keep this moment
frozen in time
hit the pause button,
suspend everything
so that I could always feel your
soft
   and
tiny hands
wrapped around my finger,
your soft breaths tickling my neck
as you sleep soundly on my chest.
I could relive every smile,
every giggle,
every beautiful coo, like wind chimes tinkling on the wind -
as my stress melted away.
But I could never do that.
Though I mourn the sense of loss,
at these cherished moments
I cannot recreate,
I embrace the excitement
of meeting who you will become,
watching as you sprout your wings
and soar to new heights -
a beautiful bird on the breeze.
My little baby bird,
growing up.

Shoulders

My shoulders are wide,
strong from
carrying the hopes of
those that have come
before me.
Wide
and sturdy enough,
for my children to
one day leap from,
towards their destiny
as they begin a journey,
like birds from the nest.

Stuck

I'm feeling stuck,
between a rock and a hard place.
I'm stuck between,
where I am and
where I'm going,
basking in the glow of
who you are now -
your chubby cheeks and little fingers
wrapping around my thumb,
and in the process, my heart.
The subtle smiles turned gentle giggles,
as you learn and grow.
But also, daydreaming of
the imperfectly perfect person,
you will eventually become.

We always look toward the destination,
losing track of the journey as it
slips past us, moving at
the speed of life.
My challenge is to treasure both -
soaking up every minute along the way,
until we reach the final destination
of who you will become.

Gentle Silence

It's during the silence
of the night, that
my heart
sings the loudest,
while you rest peacefully
in my arms -
when your gentle breaths
are a balm to slow the
racing thoughts of my mind
and I am reminded that
I am doing a great job.

Boxes

No one prepared me
for the feeling of
carefully folding clothes
that have become too tiny -
the sleeves that don't stretch enough
    and
the pant legs that
don't quite reach.
The proof that not only is
my beautiful baby growing,
but so is my heart.

No one prepared me
for the reverence I would
show
a simple onesie, once
so casually tossed into the hamper
without a care in the world.

No one prepared me
for the conflicting battle
in my mind and in my heart,
grieving the scrunch, sleepy smiles,
and other moments -
while celebrating the beautiful soul
growing in front of my very eyes..

I have an overflowing box,
as a shrine to help treasure
these priceless moments.

Here is a dedicated space for any thoughts, feelings or emotions you are feeling and want to express. You can try your hand at a poem or two, or simply make a note of something you don't want to forget. Jot down phrases that stuck with you, ideas you vibe with or anything else.

These next pages are to use however you'd like!

Remember to "feel your feels", as I like to say. Let yourself explore your emotions so you can understand them better. Sometimes putting words to paper can help you not only understand the thoughts or feelings better, but also help process them.

Try it below!

www.ingramcontent.com/pod-product-compliance
Lightning Source LLC
Chambersburg PA
CBHW010425120726
47992CB00008B/3334